CONNECT BIBLE STUDIES

All That You Can't Leave Behind

U2 (Island)

Broken World
Broken People
Happiness
Grace

www.connectbiblestudies.com

connect

linking the Word to the world

CONNECT BIBLE STUDIES: U2: All That You Can't Leave Behind

Published in this format by Scripture Union, 207-209 Queensway, Bletchley, MK2 2EB, England.

Scripture Union is a charitable organisation working around the world with the goal of making God's good news known to people of all ages and encouraging them to meet God regularly through the Bible and prayer. As well as publishing books, Bible reading notes, and a range of church resources, SU produces videos and audio cassettes, works in schools, and runs holidays, clubs and missions for children and young people.

Email: info@scriptureunion.org.uk
Internet: www.scriptureunion.org.uk

© Damaris Trust, PO Box 200, Southampton, SO17 2DL.

Damaris Trust enables people to relate Christian faith and contemporary culture. It helps them to think about the issues within society from a Christian perspective and to explore God's truth as it is revealed in the Bible. Damaris provides resources via the Internet, workshops, publications and products.

Email: office@damaris.org
Internet: www.damaris.org

ALSO AVAILABLE AS AN ELECTRONIC DOWNLOAD: www.connectbiblestudies.com

Chief editor: Nick Pollard
Consultant Editor: Andrew Clark
Managing Editor: Di Archer
Written by Di Archer, Caroline Puntis, Tony Watkins

First published 2001
ISBN 1 85999 580 2

British Library Cataloguing-in-Publication Data: a catalogue record for this book is available from the British Library.

Cover design and print production by:
CPO, Garcia Estate, Canterbury Road, Worthing, West Sussex BN13 1BW.

Other titles in this series:

And more titles following — check www.connectbiblestudies.com for latest titles or ask at any good Christian bookshop.

Using Connect Bible Studies

What Are These Studies?

These innovative home group Bible studies have two aims. Firstly, we design them to enable group members to dig into their Bibles and get to know them better. Secondly, we aim to help members to think through topical issues in a Biblical way. Hence the studies are based on a current popular book or film etc. The issues raised by these are the subjects for the Bible studies.

We do not envisage that all members will always be able to watch the films or read the books, or indeed that they will always want to. A summary is always provided. However, our vision is that knowing about these films and books empowers Christians to engage with friends and colleagues about them. Addressing issues from a Biblical perspective gives Christians confidence that they know what they think, and can bring a distinctive angle to bear in conversations.

The studies are produced in sets of four — i.e. four weeks' worth of group Bible Study material. These are available in print published by Scripture Union from your local Christian bookshop, or via the Internet at www.connectbiblestudies.com. Anyone can sign up for a free monthly email newsletter that announces the new studies and provides other information (sign up on the Connect Bible Studies website at www.connectbiblestudies.com/uk/register).

How Do I Use Them?

We design the studies to stimulate creative thought and discussion within a Biblical context. Each section therefore has a range of questions or options from which you as leader may choose in order to tailor the study to your group's needs and desires. Different approaches may appeal at different times, so the studies aim to supply lots of choice. Whilst adhering to the main aim of corporate Bible study, some types of questions may enable this for your group better than others — so take your pick.

Group members should be supplied with the appropriate sheet that they can fill in, each one also showing the relevant summary.

Leader's notes contain:

1.   Opening Questions

These help your group settle in to discussion, whilst introducing the topics. They may be straightforward, personal or creative, but are aiming to provoke a response.

2.   Summary

We suggest the summary of the book or film will follow now, read aloud if necessary. There may well be reactions that group members want to express even before getting on to the week's issue.

3.   Key Issue

Again, either read from the leader's notes, or summarised.

4.   Bible Study

Lots of choice here. Choose as appropriate to suit your group — get digging into the Bible. Background reading and texts for further help and study are suggested, but please use the material provided to inspire your group to explore their Bibles as much as possible. A concordance might be a handy standby for looking things up. A commentary could be useful too. The idea is to help people to engage with the truth of God's word, wrestling with it if necessary but making it their own.

Don't plan to work through every question here. Within each section the two questions explore roughly the same ground but from different angles or in different ways. Our advice is to take one question from each section. The questions are open-ended so each ought to yield good discussion — though of course any discussion in a Bible study may need prompting to go a little further.

5.   Implications

Here the aim is to tie together the perspectives gained through Bible study and the impact of the book or film. The implications may be personal, a change in worldview, or new ideas for relating to non-churchgoers. Choose questions that adapt to the flow of the discussion.

6.   Prayer

Leave time for it! We suggest a time of open prayer, or praying in pairs if the group would prefer. Encourage your members to focus on issues from your study that had a particular impact on them. Try different approaches to prayer — light a candle, say a prayer each, write prayers down, play quiet worship music — aim to facilitate everyone to relate to God.

7.   Background Reading

You will find links to some background reading on the Connect Bible Studies website: www.connectbiblestudies.com/

8.   Online Discussion

You can discuss the studies online with others on the Connect Bible Studies website at www.connectbiblestudies.com/discuss/

www.connectbiblestudies.com

connect

linking the Word to the world

All That You Can't Leave Behind

U2 (Island)

Part One: Broken World

'But I'm not in any way at peace. I still think the world is a really unfair and often wicked place, and beauty is a consolation prize. And it's not enough for me. It just isn't. There's always been a kind of rage in me and it does still bubble up.'
Bono, Telegraph Magazine, 28 October, 2000

Please read Using Connect Bible Studies *before leading a Bible study using this material.*

Opening Questions

Choose one of these questions.

Do you like U2's music? Why?	What is your favourite type of music and why do you like it?
What is one of your top ten favourite songs and why?	Play a U2 track and share your reactions.

Summary

Peace On Earth was written in response to the Omagh bomb of 15th August, 1998. The precarious peace in the ongoing Irish conflict was shattered by the event that killed 29 people. In an interview with CNN.com, Bono described how people listened to the names of the dead being read out over the radio. He mentions some of their names in his song. A few months later, Christmas came round once again, but that year its message seemed meaningless: 'It never sounded so out of tune, so hollow — "Peace on Earth, Goodwill to all mankind."'

His frustration and tiredness with the broken world we live in is often evident in Bono's lyrics. He talks of his feelings of dissatisfaction and anger at the randomness of death brought about by man's selfishness. He imagines the anguish of an Omagh bomb victim — 'She never got to say goodbye / To see the colour in his eyes / Now he's in the dirt' — and recognises the extent of the breakdown, as well as the solution — 'Heaven on Earth / We need it now ... / Jesus could you take the time / To throw a drowning man a line ...' *(Peace On Earth)*.

Perhaps he sees the resolution to his struggle with the broken world in terms of finding a new perspective — Bono hints at becoming like Jesus, presumably to make sense of the world: 'So I try to be like you / Try to feel it like you do' *(When I Look At The World)*.

Key Issue: Suffering in the world

U2 first appeared as we know them in 1978, inspired by the energy of punk, but wanting to say something more positive and uplifting. The band has increased in popularity ever since. Stemming from Dublin, where they were all at school together, the four members became major players on the rock scene in 1987 with their album The Joshua Tree. They won three GRAMMYs and were given a special award for their outstanding contribution to the British music industry at the 2001 Brit Awards.

In years past they have been open about their Christian faith, to which three of their members subscribe. The most famous of these is Bono. He has also spent time campaigning for justice in many contentious and painful issues facing the world today, using his celebrity status to gain publicity for them. For example, he was heavily involved in the Jubilee Campaign to persuade first world governments to drop the debts owed them by developing countries. More recently Christians have asked where the band stands now — are they still firmly on the Christian platform? It seems they are resisting direct labels these days, but what do their songs say? According to our opening quotation from Bono, does he see the world as an unfair place? What issues do they expose in their lyrics, what is important to them? Given their massive popularity, what are they saying to their fans which strikes a chord? What is their appeal?

Bible Study

The question of suffering is extremely complex and difficult. The passages below do not give a complete answer but look briefly at some of what the Bible has to say.
Choose one question from each section.

1.   **Peace on Earth?**

     Sick of sorrow / Sick of the pain / Sick of hearing again and again / That there's gonna be / Peace on Earth (Peace On Earth)

     See also Habakkuk 2:4–17; Romans 1:18–32.

     ◆   Read Ecclesiastes 4:1–4. What does the writer of Ecclesiastes say about the state of the world? Why does he say that it would be better not to have been born than to experience this?

     ◆   Read Hosea 4:1–3. This passage is addressed to the Israelites — the covenant people of God. What is God's problem with his people? How can this be applied to the world in general?

2. Stuck in a moment that you can't get out of

I wasn't jumping ... for me it was a fall / It's a long way down to nothing at all
(Stuck In A Moment You Can't Get Out Of)

This section is looking at why the world is in such a mess.

♦ Read Genesis 3:1–19. What was the fundamental temptation that Adam and Eve faced? How did the decision they took affect everything in the world?

♦ Read Romans 1:18–32. Try to summarise the sequence of stages in Paul's explanation. What is at the very heart of human sinfulness?

3. When I look at the world

[The Omagh bombing] made people bitter, obviously ... bitter not just towards the people who did it but spiritually bitter.
(Interview with Bono on CNN.com, 27 October, 2000)

♦ Read Psalm 37:1–20. Why does the Psalmist discourage anger and bitterness as a response to the state of the world? What does he recommend?

Leaders: Note that verse 4 does not mean that we can get whatever we want out of God if only we'll delight ourselves in him. Rather, if we delight ourselves in him our desires change — ultimately God himself becomes the desire of our hearts.

♦ Read Psalm 73. How does the Psalmist's response to evil in the world change? What makes the difference to him?

4. Beautiful Day

See the bird with a leaf in her mouth / After the flood all the colours came out
(Beautiful Day)

♦ Read Luke 4: 14–21. What was Jesus' response to the state of the world? What examples can you think of in the Gospels where Jesus put this into practice?

Leaders: Jesus is quoting from Isaiah 61:1–2 but cuts it short. The passage in Isaiah has 'to proclaim the year of the Lord's favour and the day of vengeance of our God.' Jesus misses out the vengeance aspect because that it not what he is proclaiming at this point in his ministry. He has come with a ministry of grace; judgment is for the future.

♦ Read Romans 5:6–19. How is the cross God's ultimate response to the problem of a broken world? In what ways does Jesus' death reverse what happened in the Fall (Genesis 3)?

Leaders: Sin and death entered the world through Adam. We are all caught up in that — we inherit a sinful nature because of Adam and we all die as a result of Adam's rebellion (though, of course, we all also make our own choice to rebel against God and deserve death because of our own sin). In the same way as we are all caught up in Adam's sin, so the possibility is open to all of us to be caught up in what Jesus Christ did to put us right with God. We are given his righteousness and access to eternal life.

Implications

If 19,000 children were dying every day in New York or Washington or London you'd call it a holocaust, but because it's Chad and Tanzania and Mozambique you don't even call it a crisis.
(Bono interviewed in Telegraph Magazine, 28 October, 2000)

Choose one or more of the following questions.

- What is so powerful about music and does it matter who sings it?

- How do you respond to the track *Peace on Earth* in the light of your discussion?

- What is your experience of 'Ecclesiastes despair' (see the discussion on Ecclesiastes 4 above)?

- Where and what is the kingdom of God? How much do we see of it here and now?

- Given the inevitability of evil after the Fall, does this mean we should not campaign against it in the world today?

Prayer

Spend some time praying through these issues.

Background Reading

You will find links to some background reading on the Connect Bible Studies website: www.connectbiblestudies.com/uk/catalogue/0003/background.htm

Discuss

Discuss this study in the online discussion forums at www.connectbiblestudies.com/discuss

Members' Sheet: All That You Can't Leave Behind — Part 1

Summary

Peace On Earth was written in response to the Omagh bomb of 15th August, 1998. The precarious peace in the ongoing Irish conflict was shattered by the event that killed 29 people. In an interview with CNN.com, Bono described how people listened to the names of the dead being read out over the radio. He mentions some of their names in his song. A few months later, Christmas came round once again, but that year its message seemed meaningless: 'It never sounded so out of tune, so hollow — "Peace on Earth, Goodwill to all mankind."'

His frustration and tiredness with the broken world we live in is often evident in Bono's lyrics. He talks of his feelings of dissatisfaction and anger at the randomness of death brought about by man's selfishness. He imagines the anguish of an Omagh bomb victim — 'She never got to say goodbye / To see the colour in his eyes / Now he's in the dirt' — and recognises the extent of the breakdown, as well as the solution — 'Heaven on Earth / We need it now ... / Jesus could you take the time / To throw a drowning man a line ...' *(Peace On Earth)*.

Perhaps he sees the resolution to his struggle with the broken world in terms of finding a new perspective — Bono hints at becoming like Jesus, presumably, to make sense of the world: 'So I try to be like you / Try to feel it like you do' *(When I Look At The World)*.

Key Issue:

Bible Study notes

Implications

Prayer

Discuss this with others on the Connect Bible Studies website: www.connectbiblestudies.com

All That You Can't Leave Behind

U2 (Island)

Part Two: Broken People

Who's to know what it is will break you
I don't know where the wind will blow
(Kite)

Please read Using Connect Bible Studies *before leading a Bible study using this material.*

Opening Questions

Choose one of these questions.

Is suffering an inevitable part of human existence?	Why do we watch so much suffering on television?
Do you like sad songs and why?	Why does our culture try to distance itself from suffering?

Summary

The broken world around us inevitably impacts on our lives in very personal ways. The pain we observe resounds in individuals with an even greater intensity — the shattering of the peace by the Omagh bomb of 1998 was felt most by the victims and their relatives: 'Tell the ones who hear no sound / Whose sons are living in the ground / Peace on Earth' *(Peace On Earth)*.

There is also the matter of pain that we cause ourselves, especially in the lives of those we love. As a rock star, Bono has spent much time away from home, perhaps in both a literal and an emotional sense. He sings about the hope of restoring a relationship that has suffered because of separation: 'In a little while — I won't be blown by every breeze' *(In A Little While)*. Instead, 'In a little while, this hurt will hurt no more / I'll be home, love'.

Bono seems to long for a time when all pain will be resolved. For now, he is '... in the waiting room / I can't see for the smoke / I think of you and your holy book / While the rest of us choke' *(When I Look At The World)*.

Key Issue: Suffering at a personal level

Suffering and pain in the world are major themes in the U2 album *All That You Can't Leave Behind*. U2 are not afraid to tackle these difficult issues in their music, and do not attempt to give slick answers. As music is such a powerful communicator, their fans must identify with the sentiments expressed.

If U2 are raising the questions, are there genuinely helpful Christian responses we can give? If U2 fans feel the pain the songs are expressing, can we meet them in it? How much do we agree with U2's perspective, and where would we want to differ? No one can deny the problem of suffering in the world, so how can we honestly and usefully approach it?

Bible Study

The question of suffering is extremely complex and difficult. The passages below do not give a complete answer but look briefly at some of what the Bible has to say.

Choose one question from each section. Each section includes one question relating to the book of Job. You may like to use these questions throughout your study or mix them with questions relating to other Bible passages.

1. Peace on Earth?

No whos or whys / No-one cries like a mother cries / For peace on Earth
(Peace On Earth)

♦   Read Job 1:13–19; 2:11–3:1; 3:20–26. What was the worst aspect of Job's suffering for him?

Leaders: We have deliberately selected three sections from the beginning of Job that focus on Job's experience, not on what was happening behind the scenes. This is all that Job knew.

♦   Read Ruth 1:1 22. What different aspects of personal suffering did Naomi and her daughters-in-law experience?

2. Stuck in a moment that you can't get out of

There's nothing you can throw at me that I haven't already heard
(Stuck In A Moment You Can't Get Out Of)

This section is exploring reasons why we experience suffering. Clearly the Bible has much more to say about this than can be covered in two brief questions.

- ◆ Read Job 4:1–11; 8:1–6. Why were Eliphaz's and Bildad's explanations for Job's suffering inadequate? What truth — if any — is there in what they said?

  See also 1:6–12; 2:1–8.

- ◆ Read 2 Corinthians 1:3–11. What explanation does Paul give for the suffering he and Timothy experienced?

3. When I look at the world

I can't wait till I'm stronger / Can't wait any longer / To see what you see / When I look at the world (When I Look At The World)

- ◆ Read Job 1:21–22; 10:1–9; 42:1–6. What are the stages Job goes through in his response to his suffering? Why?

  You might like to explore other passages in Job.

- ◆ Read Romans 5:1–5. How does the progression in verses 3–5 work? How is it different for Christians and non-Christians?

4. Beautiful Day

And if your way should falter / Along this stony pass / It's just a moment / This time will pass. (Stuck In A Moment You Can't Get Out Of)

- ◆ Read Job 19:23–27. Why is this perspective important to Job in the middle of his suffering? How does an eternal perspective affect our attitude to our suffering?

- ◆ Read 2 Corinthians 4:7–18. How does this perspective transform our approach to life's difficulties?

Implications

And I know it aches / And your heart it breaks / And you can only take so much / Walk on (Walk On)

Choose one or more of the following questions

♦ How would you talk to someone who really identifies with the pain-exposing lyrics of U2?

♦ Why do you think U2's music appeals when so much of it is about pain? What does this say about our common experience of life?

♦ What helps you when you're going through times of suffering?

♦ How important is it to have answers to the problem of suffering? Is it possible to have a final answer at all?

♦ What should we *avoid* saying to people — Christians and non-Christians — who are suffering?

Prayer

Spend some time praying through these issues.

Background Reading

You will find links to some background reading on the Connect Bible Studies website: www.connectbiblestudies.com/uk/catalogue/0003/background.htm

Discuss

Discuss this study in the online discussion forums at www.connectbiblestudies.com/discuss

Members' Sheet: All That You Can't Leave Behind — Part 2

Summary

The broken world around us inevitably impacts on our lives in very personal ways. The pain we observe resounds in individuals with an even greater intensity — the shattering of the peace by the Omagh bomb of 1998 was felt most by the victims and their relatives: 'Tell the ones who hear no sound / Whose sons are living in the ground / Peace on Earth' *(Peace On Earth)*.

There is also the matter of pain that we cause ourselves, especially in the lives of those we love. As a rock star, Bono has spent much time away from home, perhaps in both a literal and an emotional sense. He sings about the hope of restoring a relationship that has suffered because of separation: 'In a little while — I won't be blown by every breeze' *(In A Little While)*. Instead, 'In a little while, this hurt will hurt no more / I'll be home, love'.

Bono seems to long for a time when all pain will be resolved. For now, he is '... in the waiting room / I can't see for the smoke / I think of you and your holy book / While the rest of us choke' *(When I Look At The World)*.

Key Issue:

Bible Study notes

Implications

Prayer

www.connectbiblestudies.com

connect

linking the Word to the world

All That You Can't Leave Behind

U2 (Island)

Part Three: Happiness

'I'm having the best time of anyone I know. The only thing I can put up my hand and say is "At least I didn't miss it" ... I think that's my special talent. If it's going, I'm on that train.'
Bono interviewed in Telegraph Magazine, 28 October, 2000

Please read Using Connect Bible Studies *before leading a Bible study using this material.*

Opening Questions

Choose one of these questions.

What makes you happy?	Is it true that money can't buy happiness?
How do you show if you are happy?	What did happiness mean to you before you became a Christian?

Summary

Much as he denies that their latest album is autobiographical, Bono admits that it is nonetheless the product of a period of absence from responsibility on the home front. In the November 2000 issue of Q magazine, he explained, 'I *have* run off, I'm back now. I'm more at home ... with myself.' Throughout the album, Bono's lyrics have an air of Ecclesiastes about them — at the end of the day, the world does not hold all the answers.

New York symbolises the material wealth that the world has to offer. It's a busy place that entices you to come out and enjoy the way it can fill your senses. There are voices everywhere, making it difficult to hear the call to come home, but, 'In the stillness of the evening / When the sun has had its day / I heard your voice whispering / Come away now' *(New York).*

Bono was a close friend of Michael Hutchence, the former frontman of INXS, who died a popstar's death in 1997 — Bono believes that it was suicide. His death inspired him to write *Stuck In A Moment You Can't Get Out Of.* He says that it is written as an argument — the kind he wishes he could have had with Hutchence before his death. The lyrics reflect the meaningless of his pursuit of pleasure through indulgence, and its limits: 'The nights you filled with fireworks / They left you with nothing.'

Key Issue: Happiness

U2's music does not confine itself to the agony apparent in the world — it also recognises love, beauty and fun. Good relationships are celebrated and pleasure acknowledged. So their music overall communicates a range of human experience. Yet even the recognition that life is not all it could be highlights the longing for something better. So where do we find happiness in this life? Are U2's suggestions and hints valid? What indeed is happiness and where do we look for it? What is it that we are longing for?

Bible Study

1. Longing for happiness

Did I waste it? / Not so much I couldn't taste it / Life should be fragrant / Roof top to the basement (Kite)

Choose one question.

- Read Isaiah 55:1–3. What human longings does Isaiah appeal to?

- Read Luke 6:17–26. What were the people who came to Jesus looking for?

2. Looking for happiness

In New York I lost it all to you and your vices / Still I'm staying on to figure out my mid life crisis (New York)

Choose two of the following Bible passages to discuss.
Where are people looking for happiness? What are the limitations or consequences?

- Read Proverbs 6:6–11, 23–29; 23:1–5, 29–35.
  See also Proverbs 13:4; 11:4, 28; 20:1; 23:20–21; 28:7.

- Read Ecclesiastes 2:1–11.

- Read Luke 12:13–21.

- Read Galatians 5:16–21

3. Finding happiness

It's a beautiful day / Don't let it get away / It's a beautiful day (Beautiful Day)

Choose one question.

- Read Psalm 84. Where does the Psalmist find his happiness? What kind of happiness is it?

- 1 Timothy 6:6–21. How does Paul advise Timothy to live? Why is godliness with contentment great gain?

Implications

The belief that there is love and logic at the heart of the universe is a big influence on me. It's a big subject. If there is no God, it's serious. If there is a God, it's even more serious.
(Bono interviewed in Telegraph Magazine, 28 October, 2000)

Choose one or more of the following questions

♦ What is U2's perspective on happiness?

♦ Are you looking for happiness in the wrong places?

♦ Is the pursuit of pleasure always wrong? Why?

♦ Do you feel that your Christian life satisfies your deepest longings? Why?

♦ How would you seek to help a fellow Christian who seems to be focusing on the wrong things?

♦ How might you suggest to non-Christian friends that the goals of their lives are inadequate?

Prayer

Spend some time praying through these issues.

Background Reading

You will find links to some background reading on the Connect Bible Studies website: www.connectbiblestudies.com/uk/catalogue/0003/background.htm

Discuss

Discuss this study in the online discussion forums at www.connectbiblestudies.com/discuss

Members' Sheet: All That You Can't Leave Behind — Part 3

Summary

Much as he denies that their latest album is autobiographical, Bono admits that it is nonetheless the product of a period of absence from responsibility on the home front. In the November 2000 issue of *Q* magazine, he explained, 'I *have* run off, I'm back now. I'm more at home ... with myself.' Throughout the album, Bono's lyrics have an air of Ecclesiastes about them — at the end of the day, the world does not hold all the answers.

New York symbolises the material wealth that the world has to offer. It's a busy place that entices you to come out and enjoy the way it can fill your senses. There are voices everywhere, making it difficult to hear the call to come home, but, 'In the stillness of the evening / When the sun has had its day / I heard your voice whispering / Come away now' *(New York)*.

Bono was a close friend of Michael Hutchence, the former frontman of INXS, who died a popstar's death in 1997 — Bono believes that it was suicide. His death inspired him to write *Stuck In A Moment You Can't Get Out Of*. He says that it is written as an argument — the kind he wishes he could have had with Hutchence before his death. The lyrics reflect the meaningless of his pursuit of pleasure through indulgence, and its limits: 'The nights you filled with fireworks / They left you with nothing.'

Key Issue:

Bible Study notes

Implications

Prayer

www.connectbiblestudies.com

connect
linking the Word to the world

All That You Can't Leave Behind

U2 (Island)

Part Four: Grace

Grace ... a thought that changed the world
(Grace)

Please read the Using Connect Bible Studies *before leading a Bible study using this material.*

Opening Questions

Choose one of these questions.

What is the significance of 'grace' before meals? Why is it so called?	Are there any celebrities you would describe as 'grace-full'?
Jesus was described as being 'full of grace' (John 1:14). What do you think this means?	When was the last time someone was generous to you when you did not deserve it?

Summary

'The way the rot sneaks under your door is by telling you that the reason that you've had all this good fortune is because you are somehow special, rather than to make you aware that you have a gift. It is given to you in trust,' Bono commented in the November 2000 issue of *Q* magazine on the nature of success. In terms of human relationships he evidently recognises the place of grace in marriage. He admits he has been away and come home again — redeemed like the prodigal son. He sings about how it is possible to be seduced at a certain time of life in *New York:* 'I hit an iceberg in my life / But you know I'm still afloat / You lose your balance, lose your wife / In the queue for the lifeboat'.

He communicates the spiritual dimension of this idea in *Grace*, the last track of the album. Grace is personified as a woman who 'takes the blame ... removes the stain' and 'finds goodness in everything.' She 'makes beauty out of ugly things' and can change the world. Bono uses the evocative image of the making of a pearl to celebrate 'Grace' turning bad things into something beautiful.

As far as his personal salvation is concerned, Bono has confessed, 'I wish I could live up to the idea of Christianity. It's like I'm a fan; I'm not actually *in the band*.' (*Q* Magazine, November 2000).

Key Issue: Grace

We finish our studies on the issues raised by U2's music with a consideration of the lovely song Grace. The lyrics raise obvious Christian themes, as this is not just a song about a girl, but also about a concept. The grace of God is central to the Christian message and yet it remains a challenging idea for many of us. Amazing Grace is still one of the most popular hymns of all, and here Bono sings a new song about it. How does he portray it ? How well do any of us understand grace? What is it really all about?

Bible Study

Choose one question from each section. Each section includes one question relating to Ephesians 2. You may like to use these questions throughout your study or mix them with questions relating to other Bible passages.

1.   God's grace

Grace, she takes the blame / She covers the shame / Removes the stain (Grace)

♦   Read Ephesians 2:1–10. Describe in your own words the various aspects of what grace has done for us.

♦   Read Isaiah 53:4–12. Why is this passage about grace? What does grace cost?

2.   Grace v. Karma

She travels outside of karma (Grace)

Karma is the Hindu idea that we are reincarnated according to what we deserve; what we come back as depends directly on whether we have accumulated good or bad karma.

♦   Read Ephesians 2:1–10. What do we deserve? Why is grace so amazing?

♦   Read Psalm 103:8–18. Why does God not treat us as our sins deserve? Why is the fear of the Lord a liberating, gracious thing?

3. Grace in life

She carries a pearl in perfect condition / What once was hurt / What once was friction / What left a mark / No longer stains / Because Grace makes beauty / Out of ugly things (Grace)

- ♦ Read Ephesians 2:1–10. How does grace transform us from the state described in v.1–3 to that in v. 10?

- ♦ Read Romans 8:28–39. Verse 28 is often quoted to reassure Christians that everything will work out in their lives. Is this what God's grace is really all about?

4. Grace in relationships

When she goes to work / You can hear her strings / Grace finds beauty in everything (Grace)

- ♦ Read Ephesians 2:11–22. How does Paul say grace reconciles Jews and Gentiles? In what ways does this set a precedent?

- ♦ Read Matthew 18:21–35. What does Jesus' story say about the relationship between grace and justice?

Implications

Grace finds goodness in everything ... Grace finds beauty in everything (Grace)

Choose one or more of the following questions.

♦ Why do you think Bono has personalised grace in the way he has? How well does the metaphor work?

♦ What is your experience of God's grace?

♦ Why do we accept God's grace when we first come to faith but then carry on as Christians as though it's all down to us? What needs to change?

♦ Why is it sometimes hard to act with grace towards people? How can we help each other with this?

♦ How would you describe the concept of God's grace to someone who hasn't experienced it?

Prayer

Spend some time praying through these issues. You might like to allow the members of your group some space in which to pray about relationships where grace is lacking.

Background Reading

You will find links to some background reading on the Connect Bible Studies website: www.connectbiblestudies.com/uk/catalogue/0003/background.htm

Discuss

Discuss this study in the online discussion forums at www.connectbiblestudies.com/discuss

Members' Sheet: All That You Can't Leave Behind — Part 4

Summary

'The way the rot sneaks under your door is by telling you that the reason that you've had all this good fortune is because you are somehow special, rather than to make you aware that you have a gift. It is given to you in trust,' Bono commented in the November 2000 issue of *Q* magazine on the nature of success. In terms of human relationships he evidently recognises the place of grace in marriage. He admits he has been away and come home again — redeemed like the prodigal son. He sings about how it is possible to be seduced at a certain time of life in *New York:* 'I hit an iceberg in my life / But you know I'm still afloat / You lose your balance, lose your wife / In the queue for the lifeboat'.

He communicates the spiritual dimension of this idea in *Grace*, the last track of the album. Grace is personified as a woman who 'takes the blame ... removes the stain' and 'finds goodness in everything.' She 'makes beauty out of ugly things' and can change the world. Bono uses the evocative image of the making of a pearl to celebrate 'Grace' turning bad things into something beautiful.

As far as his personal salvation is concerned, Bono has confessed, 'I wish I could live up to the idea of Christianity. It's like I'm a fan; I'm not actually *in the band.*' (*Q* Magazine, November 2000).

Key Issue:

Bible Study notes

Implications

Prayer